Christian Spirituality

Group Studies

by

Paul Smith

A met Publication

Published for met
by

ISBN 978-086071-619-8
(Originally Published as 086071-580-9 in 2003)

British Library Cataloguing in Publication Data.
A catalogue record for this book is available from the British Library.

MET PUBLICATIONS

are published for MET by

Preface

Christian Spirituality

Getting Started

Christian Spirituality is the title we give to a study of the spiritual life amongst Christians. The Christian faith is supremely about a relationship with God - a spiritual relationship. The growth of this relationship requires devotion being expressed, the one to the other. God has expressed his devotion to us in the life of Jesus, and supremely through the death and resurrection of his son. We in turn, express our devotion to him. Yet the way different Christians express that devotion differs, for we all have different personalities. The things which some feel passionately about are not so important to others. The life of every local congregation would be enriched by an increasing awareness of this variety. It ought not to be seen as a threat to any individual, but an expression of the richness of Christian devotion that is open to all.

It is possible to identify 'streams' of Christian spirituality running through the church and, whilst individual Christians may identify very closely with one particular stream, their spiritual life would be deepened by an increased awareness of streams other than their own.

This short series of studies is offered in the hope that it might increase this awareness and enable each person to find new ways of thinking about God and expressing their love for him.

Paul Smith

Contents

SESSION

1. Christian Spirituality 5
2. The Life of Prayer 13
3. Social Justice 19
4. The Call to Holiness 25
5. The Spirit-filled Life 29
6. Evangelical Spirituality 33
7. Sacramental Spirituality 37

Session 1

Christian Spirituality

Not all that long ago, certainly within most of our lifetimes, science was seen as providing the answer to virtually every question. If science could not answer the question, there must be something wrong with the question! All that has changed. There is now a recognition that life consists of more than the sum total of the things you can touch, taste, feel, smell and see. Human beings too are acknowledged to be spiritual as well as physical beings.

Consequently, spirituality has become a common word in our society. Not long ago it was considered inappropriate in non-Christian circles to speak of the spiritual life. Now it has become fashionable. Spirituality is popular again.

But often, when people in secular society speak about spirituality, they mean something quite different from Christians who use that word. For the non-Christian, 'spirituality' can cover a whole range of spiritual practices from Meditation to Tarot Cards; Eastern Philosophy to Western Mysticism; Yoga to Rakei Healing; Feng Shui to Dream Catching!

It is of supreme importance therefore that at the beginning of these studies we understand what Christians mean by the word 'spirituality'. When they use the word 'spirituality' they have a far more precise understanding. For them there is a common acknowledgement that God has chosen to make himself known in Jesus. Jesus is the Way, the Truth and the Life. Christian spirituality centres around the person of Christ. It is this central emphasis on the person of Christ which makes Christian spirituality distinctive.

These studies are about *Christian* spirituality: the study and practice of the spiritual life as Christians experience it. God's definitive answer for the human race is expressed in the person of Christ. Every spirituality which does not have him as the focal point is at best a blind alley and at worst an act of deception.

- *How do members of your group feel about what has already been said? Take a moment to share together.*

Different Approaches to God

Every human being is a unique part of God's creation. No two people are the same. In the human race there is infinite variety. Physically we are different. We each have a different fingerprint and different DNA.

But the differences go deeper than just appearance. We have different ways of thinking too. Some people are very analytical, always wanting to weigh statements in the balance. Others are much more intuitive; they feel that they ought to do something and simply get on with it.

We ought not to be surprised that people are different spiritually as well. As Christians we may share the same basic beliefs; we will find them in the creeds. But when we begin to consider the devotional practices of different Christians we see that the same beliefs can lead to different kinds of Christian spirituality. A monk chanting evening prayers in a remote monastery in Eastern Europe is a far cry from a charismatic preacher pacing the stage at a Christian gathering in California, but they are both Christians, both committed to Jesus, both being used by God.

- *Take a moment in your group to share the different kinds of Christian devotion that you have seen or experienced. Maybe holidays, or other journeys abroad, have brought you into contact with different kinds of Christian Spirituality. Simply share what you have seen or shared in. How do different Christians practise the devotional life? Try to share your observations without making a value judgement on what you have seen.*

It is a most important, but very difficult, thing for many Christians to accept that other ways of approaching God may be just as valid as their own. We tend to think that we have got it right! We are more keen to share the way we see things than to learn from the approach of others. But a Christ-like soul will always be asking what we have to learn from those who are different from ourselves, for in this way we know that our own spiritual lives can be enriched. The truly Christian response, when we encounter a new way of thinking, or a new devotional practice, is really to try to understand it before we attempt to evaluate it. To condemn what we have not tried to understand does not serve the gospel; it merely reveals our own prejudices. The church would be saved from untold damage if we could begin to see the variety of spirituality as an opportunity for growth rather than a personal threat. Maybe God is wanting to enrich our experience of himself through the very people we see as being so different.

- *Can you think of examples of the way in which a lack of understanding of other Christians has led to prejudice, and prejudice has led to division and suffering?*

Variety in the local area

We don't have to travel miles to observe different kinds of spirituality. Within any small town there are Christians who share the same basic beliefs, but whose spirituality is very different. This used to be clearly identified by denominational labels. We used to have a clear understanding of how Anglicans, Baptists, Roman Catholics or Pentecostals worshipped. This is no longer the case. Within the one denomination we may have a significant variety of spiritualities. For many people today the spirituality of the local congregation is far more important than the denominational label.

Even within the local congregation there are a variety of spiritualities. Forms of worship which one person finds deeply moving can leave another cold. What enriches the spiritual life of one can leave the other unmoved. This is not because one is right and the other wrong. It is because we are all different. And we are different because that's how God made us. And we need to understand that he has brought us together into one local church congregation so that each one might be enriched by the other. Instead of feeling threatened and wanting to point out where the other person has it wrong we need to be asking what God wants to teach us through the other person whose spirituality may be very different from our own.

Discovering your own spirituality

In order to appreciate the spirituality of other people we first need to be able to understand our own spirituality a bit better. Many Christians have never really thought about it. They just do what comes naturally (or supernaturally!) - which is fine, as long as we understand that everyone else is not like us. Others may encounter God in a different way. The moment spirituality can become an adventure is the moment when we realise that there may be a richness in the spirituality of others which we have not yet discovered ourselves. So, in attempting to understand our own spirituality we are also beginning to appreciate the value of other ways to God, and maybe wondering whether we ought to try them.

Many complicated tests have been suggested to help people think about their own spirituality. Here we shall consider a simple approach. It takes into account the different ways people think about God and the different ways they find God meeting them.

Look at the diagram on the next page. The vertical axis concerns how we think about God. The horizontal axis concerns how we experience God. On the vertical axis you will see that at one extreme God is seen as a complete mystery before whom we bow in humble awe: 'God is a mystery'. At the other extreme God is entirely knowable, to whom we can speak as we would speak to any other: 'God is revealed'.

On the horizontal axis you will see, at the two extremes, two ways in which people experience God. For the one, truth is of supreme importance. Christian growth is measured by the discovery of new truth. The other person has a faith which is led by the heart, and both worship and devotion should be felt if they are to be real.

- *Try to place yourself at a point on each of these axes. The more you agree with the statement, the nearer you are to that point. Take a moment to do this and then share your findings.*

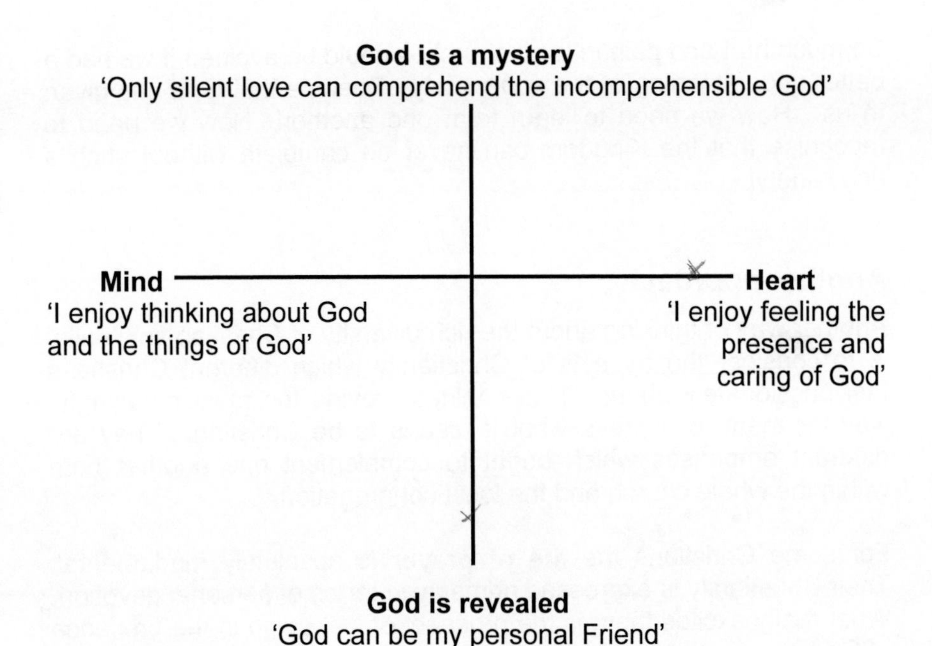

The position in which you have placed yourself on each of these lines puts you in one of the quarters.

- *Is everyone in your group in the same quarter?*

It is interesting to notice that some typical phrases fit naturally into one quarter and some into another.

- *Where would you put phrases like 'Inner Peace', 'I felt the presence of God', 'Contend for the truth as it is in Jesus' and 'Discover ways of establishing his Kingdom of justice'?*

Of course, exercises of this kind can become silly when pushed to extremes. We were not meant to be constantly analysing ourselves or one another. It is offered here as a simple way of helping us to appreciate the variety of Christian spirituality. Different Christians encounter God in different ways, but all are valid so long as they are centred in Christ.

So much hurt and pain in local churches could be avoided if we had a better understanding of the rich variety of people that God has given to us. How we need to learn from one another! How we need to recognise that the Kingdom can never be complete without such a rich variety!

Another approach

Another way of thinking about the rich diversity of Christian spirituality is to consider the aspects of Christianity which different Christians feel passionately about. These things provide the most meaningful way for them to express what it means to be Christian. They are different emphases which ought to complement one another both within the whole church and the local congregation.

For some Christians the **life of prayer** is absolutely fundamental. Their Christianity is expressed primarily in terms of personal devotion. What really excites them is the prospect of just being in the presence of God.

For others it is the idea of **living a holy life** which is of primary importance. For them the purpose of Christian living is the transformation of the individual into the likeness of Christ. This is their goal.

Others place their emphasis on **social justice** and the transformation of society. They feel deeply about injustice. They have caught a vision of a society transformed by the grace of God, living under the Lordship of Christ. Even from afar, they see the Kingdom of God.

Others emphasise the central position which **the Bible** ought to occupy in our lives. Growth in discipleship involves for them a growing understanding of the Bible. They are excited by every verse, almost every word of scripture, and call others back to its central truths.

Others stress the importance of a vital **experience of the Holy Spirit.** The heights of Christian experience are defined in terms of the movement of the Spirit, and they perceive that the great need of the church is for a new outpouring of the Spirit of God.

For others **the sacraments** are central to their faith. They could not imagine living the Christian life if they had not been baptized, and if they were prevented from partaking in Holy Communion. Further, at the heart of the sacraments is the conviction that God encounters us in the here and now through the ordinary made extraordinary. Their ideal is seeing all life as sacramental.

Of course each one of these is important. We all tend to stress the one which moves us deeply, but we need to appreciate the insights which each one has to bring. In the next few housegroup studies we will be considering some of these in greater detail in the hope that we may continue on an adventure of spiritual discovery together. In the meantime:

- *What particular spiritual emphasis of those mentioned above is central to your faith? And why?*

[9]This is how you should pray:

'Our Father in heaven,
hallowed be your name,
[10]your kingdom come,
your will be done
on earth as it is in heaven.
[11]Give us today our daily bread.
[12]Forgive us our debts,
as we also have forgiven
our debtors.
[13]And lead us not into
temptation,
but deliver us from the evil
one.'

Matthew 6

Session 2

The Life of Prayer

No one can read the story of Jesus as the Gospels record it without being impressed by the importance of prayer for him. It would be a good exercise to take a concordance and work your way through the various references to Jesus at prayer. As he was baptized by John 'he was praying' (Luke 3:21). As he prepared to choose the twelve apostles he 'spent the night in prayer' (Luke 6:12). Following an exhausting time of healing he got up early the next morning and went to a desert place and 'there he prayed' (Mark 1:35). The all-important place of prayer in his own life is clearly evident. And think of all his teaching on prayer - The Lord's Prayer and the passages which surround it (Matthew 6), the parables dealing with prayer, and the way he encouraged prayer in his followers. As his earthly ministry was drawing to its climax we find him praying for his followers and for us (John 17) and surrendering to his Father's will in the garden of Gethsemane (Luke 22:42). As he hung on the cross, he prayed for those who had nailed him there, and his dying words were a prayer (Luke 24: 36).

It was both the teaching of Jesus on prayer, and his own example, living a life of prayer, which led his disciples to make the request 'Lord, teach us to pray' (Luke 11: 1). It is interesting to remember that all the first disciples of Jesus were Jews, and as such they would have been taught prayers from infancy. Yet when they observed Jesus at prayer it is clear that they noticed a significant difference between 'praying' and 'saying prayers'. They knew how to say prayers. He knew how to pray. In him they had seen prayer as the expression of an intimate relationship with God.

Human relationships depend upon communication which is often expressed through talking to one another. When relationships go sour people say, 'We don't talk any more.'

But there is a deeper level of human relationship, the level that true lovers know, where talking seems to be unnecessary. Just to be in the presence of the other, knowing that you are completely loved and totally accepted, is enough.

When we read the Gospels and notice the emphasis that Jesus placed on prayer we are in danger of believing that he is advocating, and providing the example for, something which we *do*. That, of course, is true; but it is only half the truth. For Jesus, the life of active prayer sprang naturally from the kind of relationship he had with God.

- *Take a look at some of the ways in which this relationship is described - John 5:19, John 5:30, John 14:10.*

For Jesus the life of prayer is about far more than an activity in which he engages, however frequently. Rather it is about a quality of relationship which might best be described as intimacy. He lived so close to his heavenly Father that conversation was natural, yet not always necessary. His life was infused with the life of God.

Those whose Christian spirituality is expressed in a life of prayer remind us all that the quality of relationship with God which Jesus knew is on offer to us all. They take him as their model, and aim for a life which is lived in the presence of God.

The Way of Contemplation

This emphasis on 'being' rather than 'doing' (or to put it more correctly, 'being' before 'doing') has led many Christians to define this approach to spirituality in a distinctive way. They call it 'The Contemplative Tradition' or 'The Way of Contemplation'. For them the act of praying is simply a means of being with God, and the aim of the prayer life is constant communion with him, even when one is not engaged in the conscious act of praying.

One Christian has defined it like this:

> ".. the contemplative life is the steady gaze of the soul upon the God who loves us. It is 'an intimate sharing between friends', to use the words of St. Teresa of Avila ..... St John of the Cross defines it as 'a secret and peaceful and loving inflow of God'."

Speaking of the Contemplative Tradition, Brother Lawrence says:

> "I do nothing else but abide in his holy presence, and I do this by simple attentiveness and an habitual, loving turning my eyes on him. This I should call .... a wordless and secret conversation between the soul and God which no longer ends."

- *Spend a moment or two talking about your own experience of the life of prayer. Be honest. If you have found prayer difficult, don't be afraid to say so. What are the obstacles you encounter? Have we understood that there is a deeper level to the life of prayer in which communication, audible or not, is surpassed by the intimacy of contemplating the wonder of God and his love for us?*

As one reads those who have written about the Contemplative tradition one finds the same expressions, thought forms and often words being used again and again. They will speak of their own deep desire for God, their sense of emptiness without him, the wonder of finding him and delighting in the communion which this discovery produces. And in that communion they will speak of God's essential nature; love, peace and joy being infused within the human soul and resulting in a life which is transformed by the life of God within.

Of course, Christians seeing these truths from different perspectives may express them differently. Anyone who has been present at a prayer meeting in an evangelical church and a meeting for prayer in a church of the Catholic tradition knows that all too well. Yet in both the aim is the same - to live a life in constant communion with God, wherein his nature transforms ours. Most of our hymnbooks reflect this united aim with a diversity of expression. Interestingly, we do not often know the denomination of the hymn writers when we sing their hymns. Yet we sing the hymns, making their words our own, for they express our own longings for God which the hymn writers put much better than most of us could. To read the devotional section of most hymnbooks will reveal hymns from a rich variety of sources, yet with the common aim of helping the believer to express their desire for more of God.

- *How helpful do you find this as a way of speaking about your spiritual life? Is such a life possible for ordinary Christians at the beginning of the 21st century in the modern western world?*
- *Share any experiences you have of using the hymnbook as an aid to prayer.*

How do we do it?

This study so far may have increased our awareness of a spiritual emphasis which is new to us. So how do we begin to explore what we have discovered?

- As disciples of Jesus we need to recognise the need for spiritual disciplines. Like everything else worth having, this will demand some effort on our part.
- We need to think carefully about the practical things. When? What is the best time of the day for us? Where? Can we find a place to be alone with God, knowing that we will not be disturbed? Atmosphere - does it help to concentrate our mind if we are able to focus our eyes on something that points us to God? Does it help to hear music which reminds us of him?
- The Bible, of course, will be a great help. But many Christians read the Bible merely to gain information. That's very good, but this demands another approach. Here we read it more like a love letter than a textbook. We allow its truth to permeate our whole being. There is no rush. We don't have to complete our reading of a given passage in the day. We may want to take a story and think ourselves into it, trying to feel as the first followers of Jesus felt, when they encountered him. Or if in our reading we come across one of the great promises of scripture, we would want to pause, and take time to reflect upon it, and apply it to our own lives.
- Classic devotional literature is also very helpful. To read the devotional reflections of those who have trodden this way before us provides new insights for us who follow.

Once again, we will let their words and truth dwell in our minds, and warm our hearts, so that they become for us the gateway into the presence of God.

- Those who have practised this way of spirituality impress us with their lack of hurry. We need to learn to relax in the presence of God without feeling guilty about it, and without feeling that we desperately need to rush away to do the next thing. God made us to enjoy him, and we need to learn in stillness the joy of his presence.

Questions for Discussion

1. *What practical help would you offer to someone who said 'I can't find time to pray'?*
2. *What advice would you give to someone who said they found it very difficult to be still in a frenzied world, or to relax with God without feeling guilty?*
3. *How can we help each other to explore the life of contemplation?*

[21]"I hate, I despise your
religious feasts;
I cannot stand your
assemblies.
[22]Even though you bring me
burnt offerings and grain
offerings,
I will not accept them.
Though you bring choice
fellowship offerings,
I will have no regard for
them.
[23]Away with the noise of your
songs!
I will not listen to the music
of your harps
[24]But let justice roll on like a
river,
righteousness like a
never-failing stream!"

Amos 5

Session 3

Social Justice

Whilst the life of prayer may be the central focus for some Christians, it is social justice issues about which other Christians feel passionately. You can find such people in all branches of the Christian Church. Vincent de Paul who founded the Vincent de Paul Society; Robert Raikes, founder of the Sunday School movement; William Wilberforce who brought about the abolition of slavery in the British Empire; Elizabeth Fry who compaigned for prison reform; Lord Shaftesbury who founded the Shaftesbury Society; Florence Nightingale who pioneered nursing as we know it; Catherine and William Booth, founders of the Salvation Army; Albert Schweitzer, missionary doctor; Mother Teresa, servant of the poor; Martin Luther King Jr., campaigner for American civil rights; and Desmond Tutu, South African Archbishop – these are all Christians for whom social justice issues were of tremendous importance. They expressed their Christian faith in a world of inequality, injustice and pain. For them, following Jesus meant seeking a world which was fit for the children of God to live in.

Where did they get their inspiration for the movements they founded, or the reforms for which they campaigned? The answer is plain to see: from the pages of scripture and in particular from the life of our Lord. Any lack of understanding on our part serves only to indicate how distorted our spiritual view has been.

Throughout the Old Testament God is seen as the One who wills that his people should live in justice, freedom and peace. The prophets, especially those of the 8th century BC (Amos, Hosea, Micah and Isaiah) all had some very hard things to say about those who were keen on worship but blind to the needs of others.

- *Take a look at Amos 4:1-3, Amos 5:7-12 and Amos 5:21-24 in which God speaks out against injustice; Hosea 9:5-9 where the prophet condemns corruption; and Micah 6:6-8 where the prophet makes clear what God's requirements are.*

When we move to the New Testament, we see this same emphasis repeated. The Magnificat (Luke 1:46-56) speaks of God's activity in exalting the poor and casting down the mighty. Jesus began his ministry by reading his manifesto:

> 'The Spirit of the Lord is upon me, because he has anointed me to bring good news to the poor. He has sent me to proclaim release to the captives and recovery of sight to the blind, to let the oppressed go free, to proclaim the year of the Lord's favour' (Luke 4:18-19).

It is far too easy for us to spiritualise verses like this. If we are going to get to the heart of what Jesus meant we must try to understand what it meant to those who first heard it. For them issues of poverty, blindness, captivity and oppression were all too real. Jesus really did make blind people see. He really did bring good news to the poor. Those who were oppressed, by social stigma amongst other things, found a liberty in the affirmation which he brought. In short, Jesus set a value on ordinary people. To him everyone mattered, none was worthless.

Throughout his ministry he spoke of 'the Kingdom of God'. This is quite different from the kingdoms of this world and therefore has a different value system. In the Beatitudes he speaks of a life where the order of things is reversed and those who are despised in the world are really those who are 'blessed'.

- *Take a moment to look at the Beatitudes in Matthew 5:3-12. Notice how the qualities possessed by those who are blessed (poverty of spirit, meekness etc.) are the very qualities which are despised in the world because they are a sign of weakness.*

The Kingdom of God, announced by Jesus in his manifesto, in contrast to the kingdoms of the world, and described in the Beatitudes, was at the heart of the teaching of Jesus. We may think that this is just a kind of utopian dream, until we look at the life of Jesus. He lived like this. Indeed, in his life we see what it is like to live in God's Kingdom. Those at the bottom of the social heap were those who, apparently, mattered most to him. And those who were high on the social scale were those with whom he had the biggest problem. There can be little doubt that it was Jesus' outspoken comments about the social structures of his day which led to his initial popularity. He was someone who valued ordinary people, and cared nothing for the authority structures of his day, not least amongst religious leaders. The poor people clearly saw him as their champion. As his popularity grew he was increasingly at odds with religious and authoritarian leadership. Clearly it was this that eventually led to his death.

During the three years of Jesus' ministry his followers had begun to discover something of the life of the Kingdom. Clearly they got it wrong on several occasions, but they had glimpsed a way of living which they longed to pursue. Something wonderful happened when the Holy Spirit came in a new way at Pentecost. It is as though before Pentecost they had been trying to live out the values of the Kingdom and often failing, but after Pentecost these values became the 'natural' expression of the supernatural life of God within them. They found it quite natural to express this 'Kingdom life' in the emerging Christian community.

- *Take a look at Acts 2:42-47 and Acts 4:32-37 for a wonderful description of their life together. The values prized by the world were of no consequence to them. They had been replaced by a new set of values. How can we live by these values today?*

We do not have time in this short study to examine the New Testament letters in detail, but we need to be reminded that Paul often begins his letters by affirming profound theological truth, but concludes them by helping the first readers to understand what it means to live out that truth in the real world. He is not averse to dealing with matters such as relationships in the church, relationships with the authorities, relationships in the home, and relationships with one's employer. In all these issues he is exploring how the values of the Kingdom are expressed in a world like ours.

And the last book in the Bible holds before us a vision of a new order in which justice and righteousness prevail. It is called 'a new heaven and a new earth'. There 'mourning and crying and pain will be no more' because 'God will wipe away every tear from their eyes' (Rev 21:4).

- *How important for you are the social implications of the gospel as they are found in scripture? How do they affect the way you live?*

Those who cherish this tradition of Christian spirituality hold Matthew 22:37-40 as fundamental to their understanding of what it is to be a Christian. It is about loving God and loving one's neighbour. Further, Jesus made it plain who one's neighbour really is. Not, as was commonly accepted, the person who was culturally *equivalent*, but the one who was *different*, the Samaritan who showed compassion for a broken and bleeding Jew. He even goes on to speak of loving one's enemies and praying for those who persecute you, for they are neighbours too!

Those who advocate this tradition draw us back again and again to three important biblical words: *justice, compassion* and *peace*. They advocate these values in three different arenas of life - the life of the individual, the life of the community and the social structures within which we all live. They are driven by a vision of a world which is changed by changed people.

There is, of course, always the danger that other aspects of the Christian life - prayer, Bible study and worship - are neglected in favour of social action. But those whose teaching lies at the heart of this expression of Christian spirituality recognise how important the life of worship and devotion really is. This is what keeps the vision alive. The vision is for a world transformed by the activity of God through his people, a world which pleases him rather than breaks his heart.

Questions for Discussion

1. *Identify specific areas in the life of our nation, our communities, or in the lives of individuals where there is a lack of justice, compassion and peace.*

2. *How should Christians express their concerns about this? How could we really make a difference in one of the areas we have identified?*
3. *Share any experiences of the message we proclaim being undermined by the impression we have given of being irrelevant because Christians are not seen to make a real difference in the real world.*
4. *Do you think the social justice emphasis is an appropriate way of expressing our Christian faith today? Why – or why not?*

"[13]Therefore, prepare your minds for action; be self-controlled; set your hope fully on the grace to be given you when Jesus Christ is revealed.. [14]As obedient children, do not conform to the evil desires you had when you lived in ignorance. [15]But just as he who called you is holy, so be holy in all you do; [16]for it is written, 'Be holy, because I am holy.'

1 Peter 1

Session 4

The Call to Holiness

The word ‘holy’ finds its origin in a Hebrew word which originally meant ‘different’. The holy place was different from every other place. The holy day was to be regarded as different from other days. The holy person was different from the rest. This difference had both a negative and positive aspect. That which was ‘holy’ was different in that it was separated *from* some things and dedicated *to* others. The Temple, for example, was a holy place because what happened there was quite different from what happened in other buildings. It was dedicated to the worship of God. Maybe this is one of the reasons why Jesus became so angry when the Temple was used as a market place. In scripture that which is holy is separated, ‘distinct’ from other things of the same kind. It is dedicated to God.

Moreover, holiness is seen as being the supreme quality of God. The very word conjures up images of majesty, glory and perfection. The response of all who would come into the presence of the holy must be reverence, wonder and awe. Many have remarked that this sense of a Supreme Being who is holy, and before whom his creatures bow in awe, is at the heart of all true religion. In the Old Testament especially, ‘holiness’ can be almost frightening. The holiness of God is displayed in the cloud of his presence and the bush which is not burnt. Before him worshippers tremble and those whom he is calling remove their sandals. Isaiah’s call (Isaiah 6:1-8) is a wonderful example of the human reaction to the holiness of God.

If a sense of the holiness of God, and the human response of reverence, awe and amazement lies at the heart of all true religion, we might ask where some modern expressions of Christianity fit. In our own generation much emphasis has been placed on intimacy, closeness, and the accessibility of God. Some Christians feel that we have lost, or are in danger of losing, sight of the holiness of God.

- *Take a moment to reflect on the public worship in which you have recently shared. When was the last time you were deeply aware in worship of the holiness of God? Is there a danger that we are over familiar with God?*

In the life of Jesus we see holiness manifested in a different kind of way. Without doubt, he was holy. But in the life of Jesus the holiness of God is somehow made accessible. He is God incarnate, yet he reaches out to ordinary people in compassion. He is Emmanuel, God with us, yet he allows sinners to touch him. He was completely identified with those whom he sought to reach. Yet he was not identical to them. He was not aloof, but he was not like others. He may have changed our understanding of the holiness of God, but he was holy nevertheless - essentially different from other people. This difference consisted in that he was utterly dedicated to God's will and separate from everything that would go against it. There may have been struggle, but there was never compromise. Furthermore, he not only did the will of God, but he lived the nature of God. His followers were eventually convinced that he was God incarnate, not because they had studied theology, but because they had lived with him. His life was the life of God, so he was holy, but his holiness was expressed in purity and compassion. He was righteous, but not self-righteous.

What we see in the life of Jesus we hear in his teaching. He is the supreme advocate of righteousness. The high point of his teaching is his endorsement of the 'royal law' to love God with all our heart, soul, mind and strength and our neighbours as ourselves. The rest of his teaching is like a commentary on how that applies in different situations. So many of the parables are like illustrations of what that means in the real world. For Jesus, and for his followers, the difference is to *be* the difference which sacrificial love makes.

- *Take a look at Matthew 5:17-20. The paragraphs that follow it apply this teaching to different areas of life, especially to our relationships. Jesus takes the outward teaching of the Law and applies it inwardly to motive and intention. Is it possible to live up to Jesus' standard?*

If we were to leave it there we would do far less than justice to the teaching of the New Testament. For such a concept of holiness can be both attractive and daunting. We know what we ought to be like, but are all too aware of our shortcomings. We carry an unending burden as we feel we ought to be different, but see no way of changing except by our own effort. Such an understanding is not Christian; it is essentially Jewish.

The difference made by the Christian gospel is the difference of inward transformation. The message of the gospel concerns a change of heart. As we open our lives to the power of Christ he begins to work within and we begin to be different inside. The mind is renewed (Romans 12:1-2), affections and desires are changed (Philippians 2:5), character is transformed. The fruit of the Spirit (love, joy, peace, patience, kindness, goodness, faithfulness, gentleness, self-control - Galatians 5:22) is born on the tree of our lives. In short, when Christ comes in he begins to make us into people who are like him (2 Corinthians 5:17). And such inward transformation results in Christ-like lives, reflecting the beauty of Jesus in a world of sin, pain and darkness.

Such transformation of character is brought about not by rigorous human effort, but by the work of the Spirit within. The emphasis, therefore, ought not to be on what we do to make ourselves better, but on what we allow the Spirit of God to do within us. The key to such an understanding of Christian spirituality lies not in effort, but in surrender. Paul's great teaching on the self-less character of the Christian being modelled on the character of Christ (Philippians 2:1-11) is followed by clear teaching about how this takes place (Philippians 2:12-13). It is to be worked out in the real world. It is to be worked out with fear and trembling. Yet this working out is the result of God at work within. God's work within is to move the will, enabling the Christian to behave in a way which is in harmony with God's purposes.

Christlikeness can only be ours by keeping company with Christ, and allowing him, through his Spirit, to transform us inwardly.

- *What are the goals of the Christian life for you?*
- *Is holiness really possible in a world like ours?*

When the day of Pentecost came, they were all together in one place. [2]Suddenly a sound like the blowing of a violent wind came from heaven and filled the whole house where they were sitting. [3]They saw what seemed to be tongues of fire that separated and came to rest on each of them. [4]All of them were filled with the Holy Spirit and began to speak in other tongues as the Spirit enabled them.

Acts 2

Session 5

The Spirit-filled Life

The holiness stream of Christian spirituality focuses our attention on the power to *be*. Those who emphasise the Spirit-filled life (sometimes called the Charismatic stream of Christian spirituality) remind us of the power to *do*. Holiness concerns the transformation of character, but we must not forget that the Spirit's power enables the Christian to act in Christ-like ways.

The Spirit in the Old Testament

Christians sometimes make the mistake of thinking that God's Spirit was not at work in the Old Testament. They are wrong. It was by the Spirit that order was brought from chaos at creation (Genesis 1:2). The Spirit equips and enables prophets, priests and kings to serve God in the way that he chooses. Through the Spirit the prophets spoke the word of the Lord (e.g. Ezekiel 11:5), the prophets' words became the word of the Lord to the hearers. In Ezekiel's famous vision (Ezekiel 37:1-14) the Spirit is the one who brings life to that which is otherwise complete but dead.

It was the prophecy of Joel (Joel 2:28-29) which Peter indicated had been fulfilled on the Day of Pentecost (Acts 2). The amazing thing was that God's Spirit was now poured into the life of every believer, even servants, and Peter could see the result before him.

The Spirit in the life of Jesus

In the life and teaching of Jesus we see the essential place occupied by the Holy Spirit. At his baptism the Holy Spirit comes in the form of a dove. As Jesus begins his ministry we hear him reading 'The Spirit of the Lord is upon me...' and announcing 'Today is this scripture fulfilled in your hearing' (Luke 4:18-21). In an upper room as he prepares his followers for the imminent trauma they are to face he speaks of his going as being for the advantage of his followers (John 16:7); for his departure will enable the Holy Spirit to come, and the

Holy Spirit will be *in* them, in contrast to Jesus who is *with* them. Before he ascends to the Father the risen Christ promises the disciples 'power from on high' (Luke 24:49).

The Spirit in the Early Church

At Pentecost the believers were all 'filled with the Holy Spirit' (Acts 2:4) and the subsequent story of the Acts of the Apostles is really the story of the acts of the Holy Spirit performed through ordinary people who had been made extra-ordinary by his indwelling.

It is clear that all Christians ought to know the power of the Spirit in their own lives. Despite the fact that many had come to believe in Samaria (Acts 8:14ff), the church in Jerusalem was unwilling to allow them to go forward in their Christian lives without the Holy Spirit's power. Peter and John were despatched to minister to them. When Saul had been converted on the Damascus Road, Ananias was sent to him that he might receive his sight back, and be filled with the Holy Spirit (Acts 9:17). On discovering that the disciples at Ephesus were living below their potential, Paul asks them whether they have received the Spirit. On discovering that they had not heard that there was a Holy Spirit, he ministers to them to put the matter right (Acts 19:1-7).

Paul's letters help us to see that within the Early Church the Holy Spirit gifted people to enable them to do what was required in a strength not their own. Sometimes these were gifts which we may describe as supernatural - prophecy, healing, discernment, tongues etc. (1 Corinthians 14). Sometimes they were gifts which many of us would feel far more comfortable with - service, encouragement, etc. (Romans 12:6-8). But in each case the Apostle wants us to realise that what was being done could not be explained simply in human terms. It was the result of the followers of Christ being in-dwelt by the Spirit of God. Sometimes the impression is given that they even surprised themselves. What they did was not because of what they were, but because of who God is and the fact that he dwelt within and was working his purposes out through them. That's why they were always anxious that the credit went to him.

The Spirit in the Church Today

At the heart of this way of experiencing Christian spirituality is the reminder that Christianity is about the activity of the living God in the life of the followers of Jesus and through them into the world. It reminds us that being a Christian is not, in the last resort, about what we do; it is about what God does.

At the low points of Christian history the Christian faith has been reduced to a code of conduct, devotion has been replaced by dead liturgy and the church has become a merely human organisation wielding political power and ecclesiastical influence. At the low points in the lives of individual Christians the same can be true. That is not how it was meant to be. In our best moments we long for a sense of the presence and the power of God. We cherish a vision of a church which is alive with the life of God. We long for a world which is transformed because the followers of Jesus know a power which enables them to do what Jesus would do if he were there. In short, we long for the presence and power of the Holy Spirit. We long for God to do something.

It was this longing which, at the turn of the 20th century, gave birth to the modern Pentecostal movement. Christians in different nations were experiencing a longing for God to manifest his presence in a tangible way. Without knowing that others throughout the world were doing the same, they gave themselves to prayer that the Spirit of God would be poured out again. Their prayers were answered and small numbers of Christians in pockets throughout the world began to experience the renewing power of the Spirit. Pentecostalism was born. During the 1960's Christians in the mainline denominations began to know this same renewing power and the Charismatic Movement came to birth. Today the fastest growing branch of the Christian church is that which places an emphasis on the presence and the power of God's Spirit.

There are, of course, many critics of this emphasis within the established denominations. They will point to those who find this emphasis helpful, and accuse them of lack of reverence, lack of thinking, trivialisation, and an over-emphasis on individuality. They may have a point, but it's all too easy to lay the emphasis on the negative and miss the positive. We must not judge any emphasis in the spiritual life by the worst examples of it. Rather, let us acknowledge our hunger for God, and seek the power of God's Spirit released in our lives today, enabling us to serve him effectively.

Questions for Discussion

1. *Why do you think it is that the Pentecostal / Charismatic branch of the church is the fastest growing in our generation?*
2. *Which, if any, of the criticisms of Charismatic Spirituality do you think are justifiable?*
3. *Is there a danger that we reject this whole emphasis because we feel uncomfortable with some aspects of it?*
4. *What is God saying to his church, and to you, about being open to his Spirit's activity today?*

Session 6

Evangelical Spirituality

In modern usage the word 'evangelical' can have a variety of meanings. Sometimes it is used to describe a particular kind of worship - that which is disparagingly called 'happy-clappy' as opposed to miserably stiff! Sometimes the word is used to describe a particular kind of personality - exuberant, boisterous, even offensive. The word 'evangelical' is also often used today in a secular context, to mean one who is particularly committed to persuading others to share his or her point of view.

- *Take a moment within your group to share together what the word 'evangelical' means to you.*

In this study we are using the word with its historic meaning. By 'evangelical' we mean those who place an emphasis on the 'evangel', the Good News of the gospel. Consequently they will stress the heart of the gospel: the person of Jesus, his atoning work on the cross, the truth of the resurrection and the empowering of the Holy Spirit. Evangelicals are those for whom the Bible, because it contains this truth, is particularly important. They will always see the Bible as their first point of reference when seeking to discover God's truth for daily living as well as for salvation.

When used in this way the word 'evangelical' can embrace a wide variety of worship forms and personality groups, but they are all united in emphasising the centrality of the Bible and the saving message it contains. In continental Europe the word 'evangelical' is often used to describe those churches that emphasise the Bible over against the tradition of the church. We would call them 'Protestant'. They may have protested against false doctrine in the church, but they did so because they realised the central place which the evangel ought to occupy.

What is the gospel?

So what is this 'evangel', this good news? It is simply that all people can enter into a new abundant life with God, here and now, and that this living relationship will continue, and indeed intensify, after death. People enter this relationship, not because they are good enough, but by God's grace freely offered to them in Jesus. In the person of Jesus the doors into God's kingdom are flung wide open and anyone can enter. Those who do so enter it by faith. They know that they are undeserving, but take God at his word. They trust him, and those who enter deepest into this new life trust him *alone.*

Sometimes, in order to help other people understand how to become a Christian, evangelicals have taken a number of proof texts in a particular order. You may want to look these up now, and trace the progression of thought:

Romans 3: 23
Romans 6: 23
Romans 5: 8
John 3: 16
Revelation 3: 20

- *In twos in your group, share with one another how you would answer the question 'What is the gospel?' After a little while, share your reflections with the whole group.*

The overwhelming sense of the new life offered freely through Jesus lies at the heart of evangelical spirituality. Evangelical Christians are constantly amazed by the grace of God. The sense of undeserved love, with all that love offers, moves them deeply and fashions their basic understanding of what it is to be a Christian. To them it seems a scandal that so many live without knowing of this love, so they are keen to proclaim the evangel. For them worship is an expression of praise and thanks for God's grace, so it is deeply personal. Their daily devotional habit will centre on the scriptures, for there they will see this love gloriously displayed. They know that life, in order to be fulfilling, must be lived against the backdrop of God's grace.

Our understanding of Christian spirituality is, of course, influenced by our history. At particular times in the history of God's people there has been new stress on the heart of the gospel with its emphasis on the grace of God. Such periods, often termed Revivals, have resulted in phenomenal and rapid growth in the church. Because such periods were accompanied by a new emphasis on the evangel, they are often termed 'evangelical revivals'.

It is not surprising that a new and deep awareness of the undeserved love of God, freely offered in Jesus, stirs the heart. Here we can identify another feature of evangelical spirituality. For an evangelical, the Christian faith concerns both mind and heart. They believe with the mind, but the wonder of what they believe stirs the heart. They practise their faith acknowledging that both mind and heart matter. At its best, evangelical spirituality preserves both these aspects of the truth, and holds them in a sometimes precarious balance. To attend worship in an evangelical church ought both to feed the mind and warm the heart, if the balance has been preserved.

This is not to say that all evangelical worship is the same. For some, set order is really important. For others, freedom of expression takes priority. For some, the hymns that shaped the church are crucial. For others, modern worship songs are the most appropriate expression of faith. Yet for all evangelicals worship ought to stir the heart as well as feed the mind.

The first Evangelical Revival, under the ministries of George Whitfield and John and Charles Wesley, transformed British society and radically re-shaped the church. Methodism, initially a body of people seeking renewal within the Church of England, later became a denomination in its own right. John Wesley, its human founder, was the epitome of an evangelical: grounded in scripture, with a deeply personal faith and a zeal which sent him to share the good news with all who would receive it. The original emphases of Methodism are sometimes summed up in what we call the four 'Alls' of Methodism:

- All people need to be saved
- All people can be saved
- All people can know they are saved
- All people can be saved to the uttermost

Ours is good news for everyone, and there is no limit to what God's grace can do in the life of each person who takes Christ seriously.

We are, of course, aware of the dangers. Those who emphasise the written word can become inflexible and intolerant of others. Those who know a zeal for the gospel can become aggressive, and even offensive, simply because they feel things deeply. Evangelicals can be more concerned about guarding truth than sharing love. But despite all these pitfalls evangelicalism has much to teach us and much to enrich the life of the church.

Questions for Discussion

1. *Which is most important in the Christian life, what we do, or what God does?*
2. *Is the heart as important as the mind in your Christian faith?*
3. *How comfortable do you feel to be described as 'evangelical'?*
4. *What are the major strengths and weaknesses of evangelical Christianity?*

Session 7

Sacramental Spirituality

Like the word 'evangelical', we need to be clear about what we mean by the word 'sacramental' in the context of Christian spirituality. A sacrament, in the way we are understanding the word, is a way of making present and visible the life of the Spirit. It is a silent, yet powerful, proclamation of the grace of God.

Through Baptism, for example, we see before us the accepting love of God proclaimed. The water speaks of the cleansing which he offers, and the promises made remind us of the responsibilities which must accompany the acceptance of such love. Baptism, therefore, as a sacrament points us beyond the physical things to the realms of the Spirit; beyond the actions and words and water to the inviting, renewing, but demanding grace of God.

Holy Communion is equally powerful in its proclamation of God's grace. At its institution Jesus, meeting in an upper room with his disciples, took bread and clearly said 'This is my body which is for you' (1 Corinthians 11:24). Imagine how the disciples felt when, after making that statement, he passed it round to them. When the supper was over, he took a cup of wine. 'This cup is the New Covenant in my blood', he said, and then invited them to drink it.

The followers of Jesus in different denominations have not always agreed with one another when they have spoken about this bread and wine. But they are all agreed that they become different. It is not just any piece of bread or glass of wine any more. They are physical things, but they point beyond themselves to spiritual truth. Bread broken and offered speaks of self-giving love. It is, as Paul says, a proclamation of the Lord's death until he comes.

In the sacraments the association between physical things and the spiritual truths of which they speak is so powerful that some find it impossible to distinguish between the two. To be baptised is to be accepted by God and to accept him, they assert. To receive bread and wine is to receive grace. Other people speak of water, bread and wine simply as symbols for something much deeper. For them the distinction, lost on others, is very important.

Much discussion, and division, in the church has been centred around the relationship between the physical things used in the sacraments and the spiritual truth, the grace, of which they speak.

- *How closely do you associate the physical things - water, bread and wine - with the grace which they proclaim? Are they merely symbols, or does receiving the one mean that one automatically receives the other?*

However we understand the sacraments we need to hold onto the core truth we are discovering. A sacrament is that which makes manifest and visible the realm of the Spirit, the grace of God. This understanding is crucial as we consider sacramental spirituality, and it is for this reason that sometimes this kind of spirituality is called incarnational. God makes himself known through real and tangible things. God is manifest through material means.

The world of the Spirit and the world of the material are not in opposition to one another. They are complementary. God created the material, physical world. This is the world in which we live. It is here that we are called into a relationship with God, and it is in the material and physical world that we are called to manifest his life. Sacramental and incarnational spirituality challenge us to change our view of daily living.

The sacraments are not just things that Christians do, however important they may be. They are models for Christian living. God's love and saving purposes are made tangible through material things. Once this truth shapes our understanding it opens up the possibility of the whole of Christian life being sacramental, every act of service pointing people beyond itself to the love of God. The life of God is made real and tangible, is incarnated, through the life of every Christian.

Of course, Jesus is the supreme example of this incarnational life.

- *Take a look at Philippians 2:6-8 to see how Paul describes it.*

We see ample evidence of this truth as we read the Gospels. As folk encountered him they knew the presence of God; yet more importantly for our study, they encountered the life of God when he was doing ordinary as well as extraordinary things. The life of God was present in the market place as well as in the miracle, in the home as well as in the healing. And we would do well to remember that Jesus spent 18 years working in a carpenter's shop. He was God incarnate there too. All life was transformed by his presence.

- *If you had gone to his carpenter's shop in Nazareth some time during those 18 years how do you think it would have been different from other carpenter's shops?*
- *Now take a look at 2 Corinthians 4:6-12 to see how Paul sees this truth working out in our lives.*

Such an emphasis reminds us that all life belongs to God. It is not as though matter is bad, or a necessary evil, and spirit is good. The earth is the Lord's and every good thing can have a sacramental dimension, manifesting the presence of God like bread and wine. There is a sacrament of daily living, in which his presence and grace are made tangible through real, material things. The way we see our work can be transformed, for everything can point towards him. And such a view can transform our attitude to the creation of which we are a part.

We are all called to this sacramental living, seeking to make present and visible the realm of the invisible Spirit and the truth of God's grace. Yet because many of us may not have grown up with a strong emphasis on this approach we need to ask God's help. When you encounter a new situation ask him to show you how he wants to make himself known through it. Take time to review the whole parcel of your life before him and consider what you need to do to enable the presence of God to be more clearly visible in your ordinary daily living. Pursue this way of thinking so that the mystery of God's presence may be seen as clearly in the 'trivial round, the common task' as it is in the water of Baptism or the bread and wine of Holy Communion.

Questions for Discussion

1. *Why do you think it can be dangerous to divide our lives into the sacred and the secular, the spiritual and material, and to live in two separate compartments?*
2. *Share together what the Sacraments mean for you. How would you help someone who wanted to get past the physical and tangible to the spiritual truth?*
3. *Take time to reflect and share together how God's love is already being made real in your home, your place of work, your social life and your church.*
4. *Do you agree with the statement 'Being a Christian is just a matter of living out what it means to be the person God has made you'?*